ALIVE

Academic Learning Integrated with Values Education

A Comprehensive Guide to Value Formation Across All Learning Groups

Inspired by Romans 8 -...the spirit is ALIVE because of righteousness.....

By

Dr. Bernardo C. Lunar

Dr. Ma. Socorro M. Eala

By Dr. Bernardo C. Lunar & Dr. Ma. Socorro M. Eala

ISBN:

Hardbound-978-621-470-798-0

Softbound/Paperback-978-621-470-799-7

PDF (downloadable)-978-621-470-800-0

Published by:
Poetry Planet Book Publishing House
Rosario, Pozorrubio, Pangasinan,
Philippines Contact Number: 09554960094
Email: maritesritumalta@gmail.com

TABLE OF CONTENTS

ABOUT THE BOOK

Welcome to "**ALIVE: A**cademic **L**earning **I**ntegrated with **V**alues **E**ducation**:** A Comprehensive Guide to Value Formation Across All Learning Groups" This book is designed to be a trusted companion for educators, parents, and all those passionate about shaping the next generation. Here, we embark on a journey that explores the importance of values education and provides practical strategies for fostering values in learners of all ages.

Adopting the thematic instruction across the different subjects and courses, values education is not made as a mere addition to the curriculum; it is designed to be the bedrock upon which individuals can build their lives. It empowers students to navigate the complexities of the world, make sound ethical decisions, and develop empathy and compassion for others. By integrating values education across grade levels, we can lay a strong foundation that equips students with the necessary skills to lead purposeful and fulfilling lives.

This book takes a holistic approach, recognizing that values education encompasses not only the classroom but also the home and the wider community. It draws on research, practical insights, and the experiences of educators and experts from diverse backgrounds. By embracing this comprehensive approach, we can create a seamless continuity in values education, reinforcing and deepening the lessons learned as learners progress through different grade levels.

Throughout this guide, we will explore a wide range of topics, including the importance of cultivating core values, strategies for fostering values in early childhood, effective teaching methodologies for different age groups, and the role of character development in building ethical leaders. We will also delve into ways and activities that can be readily implemented in classrooms and homes.

Ultimately, our goal is to empower educators and parents to shape values-driven learning environments that inspire students to become responsible, compassionate, and engaged citizens of the world. By nurturing values across grade levels, we can create a positive ripple effect that extends far beyond the walls of a classroom, impacting individuals, communities, and society at large. As we embark on this journey together, let us remember that values education is a lifelong pursuit. It requires commitment, collaboration, and an unwavering belief in the potential of every learner. By investing in their values, we invest in a brighter future for all. So, let us begin this transformative exploration into values education across grade levels, and together, let us sow the seeds of a better world.

I

Values Education For All Learners

Values education for the young is essential for their holistic development and the building of a strong foundation for their future. It involves teaching children about moral, ethical, and social values that will guide their behavior, decision-making, and interactions with others. Here are some key aspects of values education for SPC learners:

Character Development: Values education helps develop strong character traits such as honesty, integrity, empathy, respect, responsibility, and fairness. These qualities enable children to become well-rounded individuals who can make positive contributions to society.

Moral and Ethical Awareness: Teaching learners about moral and ethical principles helps them understand the difference between right and wrong. They learn to make ethical choices, consider the consequences of their actions, and develop a sense of accountability.

Respect for Diversity: Values education promotes acceptance and respect for diversity in all its forms, including race, culture, religion, gender, and abilities. Young children should learn to appreciate and celebrate differences, fostering inclusivity and reducing prejudice.

Empathy and Compassion: Nurturing empathy and compassion in children allows them to understand and share the feelings of others. It encourages kindness, generosity, and the willingness to help those in need.

Responsible Citizenship: Values education instils the importance of being an active and responsible citizen. Children learn about their rights and responsibilities, democratic principles, environmental stewardship, and global citizenship.

Critical Thinking and Decision-Making: Values education encourages children to think critically, analyze situations, and make informed decisions based on their understanding of ethical values. This skill empowers them to navigate complex moral dilemmas they may encounter.

Conflict Resolution and Communication Skills: Children need to learn effective communication and conflict resolution skills to handle disagreements and disputes peacefully. Values education teaches them negotiation, compromise, active listening, and the art of respectful dialogue.

Personal Well-being and Mental Health: Values education emphasizes the importance of self-care, mental health, and emotional well-being. Children learn about self-esteem, resilience, coping mechanisms, and maintaining a healthy balance in their lives.

Family and Community Values: Values education recognizes the influence of families and communities in shaping a child's values. It encourages collaboration between parents, educators, and the wider community to reinforce consistent messages and provide positive role models.

Ethics in the Digital Age: With the prevalence of technology, values education should include digital ethics. Children need to understand responsible online behavior, cyberbullying prevention, digital privacy, and the consequences of their digital actions.

To effectively implement values education, it is important to adopt a holistic and interdisciplinary approach that integrates these values into various aspects of a learner's life, including curriculum, school culture, classroom activities, and parental involvement. By prioritizing values education for the young, we can contribute to the development of a generation that upholds positive values and contributes to a better society.

II

Value Formation at Home

Value formation at home is a crucial aspect of a child's upbringing and plays a significant role in shaping their character and moral compass. Here are some ways to foster value formation at home:

Leading by Example: Children learn a great deal by observing their parents and caregivers. It's important for adults to model the values they want to instil in their children. Be mindful of your behavior, actions, and choices, as children often emulate what they see.

Keeping Open Communication Lines: Encourage open and honest communication with your child. Create a safe and supportive environment where they feel comfortable discussing their thoughts, feelings, and moral dilemmas. Engage in conversations that promote critical thinking and ethical decision-making.

Teaching Empathy and Kindness: Help your child develop empathy by teaching them to understand and share the feelings of others. Encourage acts of kindness and teach them to consider the impact of their actions on others. Empathy and kindness are foundational values that foster positive relationships and a caring attitude towards others.

Setting of Clear Expectations and Boundaries: Establish clear expectations and boundaries regarding behavior, respect, and responsibilities. Consistently reinforce these expectations and hold your child accountable when they deviate from them. This helps them understand the importance of values and the consequences of their actions.

Moral Storytelling: Share moral stories, fables, and parables that highlight important values and ethical lessons. Discuss the stories together, asking questions that encourage reflection and critical thinking. Use these stories as a springboard for conversations about values and their practical application.

Engaging in Family Activities: Participate in activities as a family that promote values such as cooperation, teamwork, and respect. This can include volunteering together, participating in community service projects, or engaging in creative endeavors that foster collaboration and mutual respect.

Encouraging Responsibility and Independence: Give your child age-appropriate responsibilities that allow them to develop a sense of accountability and independence. Teach them the importance of taking care of their belongings, completing chores, and contributing to the family or community in meaningful ways.

Practicing Mindfulness and Reflection: Teach your child the importance of self-reflection and mindfulness. Encourage them to think about their actions and how they align with their values. Provide opportunities for them to pause, evaluate their choices, and make any necessary adjustments.

Fostering Respect for Differences: Celebrate diversity within your family and encourage respect for differences. Teach your child about various cultures, religions, and perspectives. Help them develop an appreciation for diversity and empathy towards others who may be different from them.

Encouraging Critical Thinking: Stimulate your child's critical thinking skills by engaging them in discussions about moral and ethical issues. Encourage them to question and analyze different perspectives, consider the consequences of actions, and make informed decisions based on values.

Remember that values are best learned through consistent reinforcement and positive reinforcement. Be patient and supportive as your child develops their understanding of values. By actively promoting value formation at home, you can contribute to raising morally responsible and compassionate individuals.

III

Values formation in Schools

Value formation in schools is a vital aspect of education that complements the academic curriculum. Schools have the unique opportunity to create a nurturing environment where students can develop strong values, ethics, and character. Here are some ways in which schools can foster value formation:

Values Integration: Schools should integrate values education across the curriculum, infusing values into various subjects and activities. This helps students see the practical application of values in real-life situations and fosters a holistic understanding of values.

Positive School Culture: Schools should cultivate a positive and inclusive culture that promotes respect, empathy, and cooperation. This can be achieved through creating supportive relationships between students, teachers, and staff, as well as fostering a sense of belonging and community.

Ethical Role Models: Schools should provide students with ethical role models, including teachers, administrators, and staff who exemplify the values being taught. These role models can inspire students through their words and actions, serving as guides in the formation of values.

Character Education Programs: Schools can implement specific character education programs that focus on cultivating values such as honesty, integrity, empathy, responsibility, and respect. These programs can include structured lessons, activities, and discussions that actively promote character development.

Service Learning: Engaging students in service-learning projects and community service activities can instil values such as compassion, social responsibility, and civic engagement. These experiences provide students with opportunities to apply their values in meaningful ways and make a positive impact on the community.

Moral Dilemma Discussions: Teachers can facilitate discussions on moral dilemmas and ethical issues, allowing students to critically analyze different perspectives and make ethical decisions. These discussions promote critical thinking, empathy, and the development of a moral compass.

Peer Mediation and Conflict Resolution: Schools should teach students effective communication and conflict resolution skills, empowering them to resolve conflicts peacefully and respectfully. This helps develop values such as empathy, active listening, and compromise.

Appreciation of Diversity: Schools should foster an appreciation for diversity and multiculturalism. By celebrating and respecting different cultures, religions, and backgrounds, students learn the values of tolerance, acceptance, and inclusivity.

Mindfulness and Social-Emotional Learning: Schools can incorporate mindfulness practices and social-emotional learning programs that help students develop self-awareness, emotional intelligence, and empathy. These practices contribute to the formation of values related to well-being, mental health, and interpersonal relationships.

Parental Involvement: Collaboration between schools and parents is essential in values formation. Schools should actively involve parents in discussions, workshops, and activities that promote values education, ensuring a consistent message is reinforced at home and in school.

Schools play a crucial role in shaping the character, values, and ethics of young individuals. By incorporating comprehensive values education into their curriculum and creating a positive school culture, schools can contribute to the development of responsible, compassionate, and ethical citizens.

IV

San Pablo Colleges' Values Formation Framework

San Pablo Colleges' Value Formation Framework integrates various elements such as SPC core values, expected graduate attributes, global citizenship education, sustainable development goals (SDGs), and social innovation fundamentals. This provides a comprehensive and developmental approach to nurturing values among its students.

Guided by the Value Formation Framework, academic departments and support offices shall strive to integrate and synergize to implement such formation initiative. In an orchestrated manner, all stakeholders should seek opportunities for integration and synergy among the various value elements. The thematic curriculum integration of these values has to be coupled with experiential earning experiences and reflection activities.

Figure 1. Framework of San Pablo Colleges Curriculum Integration of Values Education

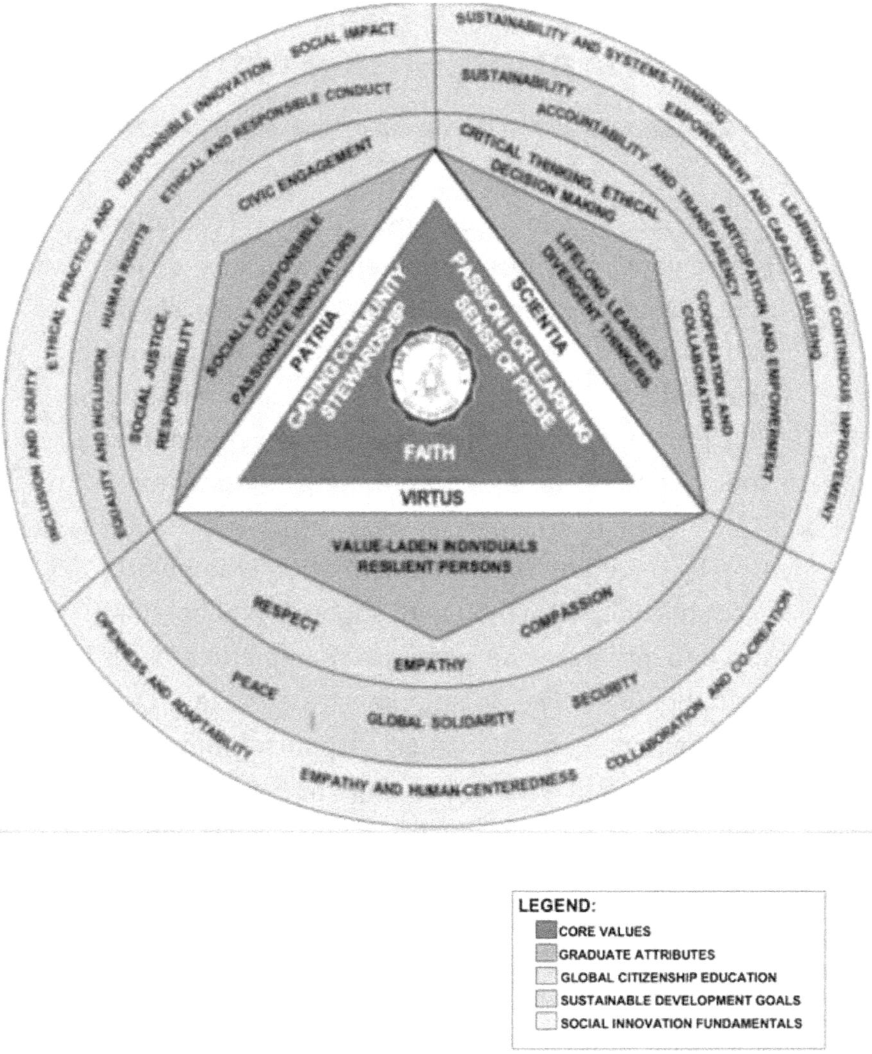

SOCIAL IMPACT
ETHICAL PRACTICE AND RESPONSIBLE INNOVATION
INCLUSION AND EQUITY
ETHICAL AND RESPONSIBLE CONDUCT
HUMAN RIGHTS
EQUALITY AND INCLUSION
CIVIC ENGAGEMENT
SOCIAL JUSTICE
RESPONSIBILITY
SOCIALLY RESPONSIBLE CITIZENS
PASSIONATE INNOVATORS
SUSTAINABILITY AND SYSTEMS-THINKING
SUSTAINABILITY
EMPOWERMENT AND CAPACITY BUILDING
LEARNING AND CONTINUOUS IMPROVEMENT
ACCOUNTABILITY AND TRANSPARENCY
PARTICIPATION AND EMPOWERMENT
CRITICAL THINKING, ETHICAL DECISION MAKING
LIFELONG LEARNERS
DIVERGENT THINKERS
COOPERATION AND COLLABORATION
PATRIA
SCIENTIA
VIRTUS
CARING COMMUNITY
STEWARDSHIP
PASSION FOR LEARNING
SENSE OF PRIDE
FAITH
VALUE-LADEN INDIVIDUALS
RESILIENT PERSONS
RESPECT
COMPASSION
EMPATHY
PEACE
GLOBAL SOLIDARITY
SECURITY
OPENNESS AND ADAPTABILITY
EMPATHY AND HUMAN-CENTEREDNESS
COLLABORATION AND CO-CREATION

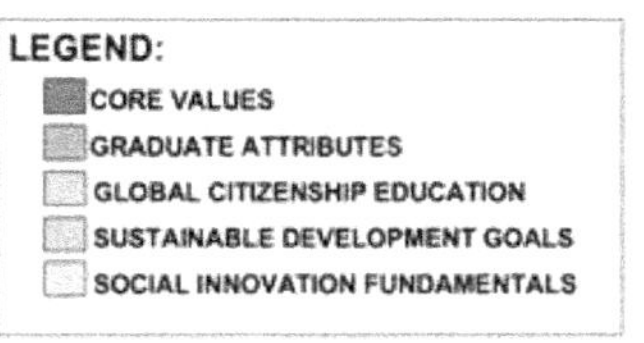

Opportunities for community engagement, service-learning projects, internships, and partnerships with organizations need to be provided. Students should be encouraged to reflect on their experiences and connect them to the core values and graduate attributes.

Assessment and evaluation strategies must align with the value formation framework. Educators should use a mix of formative and summative assessments to evaluate students' understanding of the core values, application of graduate attributes, engagement in global citizenship initiatives, and integration of social innovation principles. Assessment methods such as portfolios, reflective journals, presentations, and project-based assessments should be employed.

A regularly review and refinement the value formation framework based on feedback, evaluation results, and emerging best practices must be done. Likewise, professional development opportunities for educators are needed in order to deepen their understanding of the framework's components and pedagogical strategies, enabling them to effectively support students' value formation journey.

Furthermore, fostering of partnerships with external stakeholders, including parents, local communities, businesses, NGOs, and government agencies is a must to engage them in supporting and reinforcing the values and principles of the framework. Collaboration with these stakeholders will facilitate the provision of authentic learning experiences, mentorship opportunities, and resources that enhance students' understanding and application of values.

By anchoring the value formation framework on SPC core values, expected graduate attributes, global citizenship education, sustainable development goals, and social innovation fundamentals, you can provide a holistic approach to nurturing students' values and equipping them with the knowledge, skills, and mindset needed to contribute positively to society and address global challenges.

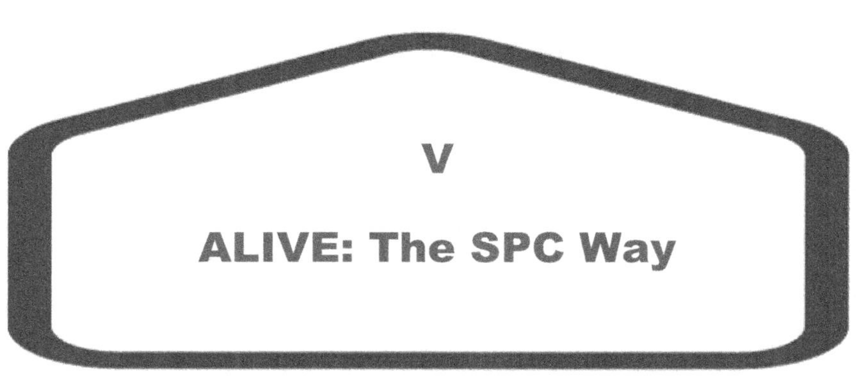

V

ALIVE: The SPC Way

Integrating a school's core values and expected graduate attributes into values education provides a strong foundation for students' character development and holistic growth. Here's how San Pablo Colleges intends to effectively execute ALIVE:

Articulating the Core Values: Identified the core values that define the school's ethos and culture that align with the school's mission and vision are clearly articulated. These values well communicated to students, staff, and parents, emphasizing their importance in shaping the school community.

Thematic Integration of Values Across the Curriculum: Infuse values education throughout the curriculum, ensuring that each subject area provides opportunities for students to understand and practice the core values. For example, if the core value is respect, teachers can incorporate activities and discussions in various subjects to explore respectful behavior in different contexts.

Development of a Values Framework: Create a values framework that outlines specific behaviors and attitudes associated with each core value. This framework can serve as a guide for teachers and students in understanding and applying the values in their daily lives. Regularly revisit and reinforce the framework through discussions, reflections, and real-life examples.

Promoting Reflection and Discussion: Provide regular opportunities for students to reflect on their personal values and how they align with the school's core values. Encourage open discussions where students can share their perspectives, ask questions, and explore ethical dilemmas. These activities foster critical thinking, empathy, and a deeper understanding of values.

Providing Opportunities for Service-Learning and Experiential Learning: Incorporate service-learning projects, community engagement, and experiential learning opportunities that allow students to apply the core values in real-life contexts. These experiences provide practical examples of how values shape relationships, decision-making, and community contributions.

Explicit Teaching of Expected Graduate Attributes: Clearly define the expected attributes or qualities that the school aims to develop in its graduates. These attributes may include qualities like resilience, leadership, adaptability, and global citizenship. Explicitly teach and reinforce these attributes alongside the core values, helping students understand their importance and relevance.

Fostering Student Leadership and Engagement: Empower students to take ownership of values education through student leadership programs, clubs, or committees focused on promoting and exemplifying the core values. Provide opportunities for student-led initiatives that reinforce the values and expected graduate attributes within the school community.

Forging Collaborative Partnerships: Collaborate with parents, families, and the wider community to reinforce the school's core values and expected graduate attributes. Engage parents in discussions, workshops, and activities that promote values education, creating a unified approach between home and school.

Celebrating and Recognizing Values-Based Behaviors: Acknowledge and celebrate instances where students demonstrate the core values and expected graduate attributes. Implement recognition programs, certificates, or awards that highlight and appreciate students' ethical and values-driven actions.

Monitoring and Continuous Evaluation and Improvement: Regularly evaluate the effectiveness of values education initiatives by collecting feedback from students, parents, and staff. Use this feedback to refine and improve the values education programs, ensuring they remain relevant, impactful, and aligned with the evolving needs of the school community.

By integrating a school's core values and expected graduate attributes into values education, schools can create a cohesive and purposeful approach to character development. This integration helps students develop a strong moral compass, personal integrity, and the skills necessary to navigate the complexities of life with ethical decision-making.

VI

Integrating SPC Core Values Across Curricula

Together with the vision and mission of the school, core values play a crucial role in shaping the culture, environment, and overall success of schools. They serve as guiding principles that influence the attitudes, behaviors, and decision-making processes within the educational institution. ore values serve as the moral compass and foundation of a school. They provide a shared understanding of what the school stands for, guide decision-making, shape the culture and climate, foster ethical and moral development, engage the community, and promote character education. By integrating core values into all aspects of school life, educators can create an environment that nurtures the growth and success of students academically, socially, and emotionally.

SPC CORE VALUES

Faith

Fidelity to and being grounded in the faithfulness of God, realizing that there is more to life thereby committing their lives in the service of mankind and the salvation of souls.

Key Behavioral Indicators for learners: humble, gentle, patient

Stewardship

Willingness to shape services to meet the changing needs of all learners and stakeholders, thus, making significant contributions to the larger community.

Key Behavioral Indicators for learners: diligent, persistent, hardworking

Passion for Learning

Strong and harmonious engagement among learners considers everyone as self-determined individuals who are capable of recreating themselves to improve teaching and learning.

Key Behavioral Indicators for learners: independent, driven, dedicated

Caring Community

Expression of genuine relationship between self and others, thus, inspiring and sharing one's success and significance with the larger community that goes beyond giving respect to the worth and dignity of all

Key Behavioral Indicators for learners: respectful, trustworthy, responsible

Sense of Pride

Delighting in one's success and continuously seeking for challenging experiences, while enhancing one's feelings of pride and self-worth and staying connected and proud of being identified as an SPCian.

Key Behavioral Indicators for learners: grateful, confident, loyal

VII

Integrating Graduate Attributes Across Curricula

The integration of the graduate attributes is crucial to ensure that their graduates are well-prepared for the demands of the future. It ensures that the quality of education it provides to all its learners remains relevant and practical. Further, it engages students, fosters holistic development, ensures quality assurance, and aligns with the expectations of stakeholders.

Expected SPCian Graduate Attributes

VIRTUS

Value Laden Individuals - heeding the call to lead, protect, and provide both physically and spiritually through the pursuit of righteousness, godliness, faith, love, steadfastness, and gentleness.

Key Behavioral Indicators for learners: honest, kind, loving

Resilient Persons - realizing that there is greater joy and satisfaction ahead by successfully adapting to difficult and challenging life experiences and demands.

Key Behavioral Indicators for learners: adaptive, courageous, optimistic

PATRIA

Socially Responsible Citizens - committing to work and cooperate with other individuals and organizations for the benefit of the community that will inherit the world that individual leaves behind.

Key Behavioral Indicators for learners: patriotic, responsible, socially aware

Passionate Innovators - manifesting innovations and discourses in the discipline for implementation, monitoring and evaluation purposes indicative of one's high leadership performance.

Key Behavioral Indicators for learners: adept, creative, skillful

SCIENTIA

Lifelong Learners - upholding the love to make progress and staying open to changes and new perspectives while seeking new opportunities towards common goals and objectives.

Key Behavioral Indicators for learners: motivated, competitive, enthusiastic

Divergent Thinkers - contributing to the professional advancement through continuous quest for knowledge by taking an active stance in research and development.

Key Behavioral Indicators for learners: inquisitive, critical, smart,

VIII

Integrating Values from Global Citizenship Education in the High School Curriculum

Integrating global citizenship in the curriculum is essential to prepare students to become responsible, informed, and engaged global citizens. By integrating global citizenship in the curriculum, educational institutions can foster students' global awareness, cultural competence, critical thinking, empathy, and a sense of responsibility towards the world. This equips them with the knowledge, skills, and attitudes necessary to navigate and contribute to an interconnected and interdependent global society.

Global citizenship education is rooted in a set of values that help shape students' understanding of their role as active global citizens. Here are some values commonly embedded in global citizenship education:

Respect: Global citizenship education emphasizes respect for the dignity, rights, and perspectives of all individuals, regardless of their cultural, ethnic, religious, or socio-economic backgrounds. It promotes an appreciation for diversity and fosters an inclusive and equitable environment where all voices are valued and heard.

Social Justice: Global citizenship education encourages a commitment to social justice and the promotion of fairness, equality, and human rights. It addresses issues of inequality, poverty, discrimination, and marginalization at local, national, and global levels. It empowers students to take action against injustices and work towards creating a more just and equitable world.

Responsibility: Global citizenship education instills a sense of responsibility towards the well-being of others and the planet. It encourages students to recognize the impact of their choices and actions on local and global communities. It promotes sustainable practices and encourages students to contribute to positive social and environmental change.

Empathy and Compassion: Global citizenship education cultivates empathy and compassion by developing students' ability to understand and appreciate the experiences, perspectives, and challenges of others. It encourages students to consider the broader implications of their actions and to show care and concern for others, both near and far.

Critical Thinking: Global citizenship education fosters critical thinking skills, enabling students to analyze complex global issues, challenge biases and stereotypes, and evaluate different sources of information. It encourages students to think critically about the root causes of global challenges and to develop informed opinions based on evidence and multiple perspectives.

Cooperation and Collaboration: Global citizenship education emphasizes the importance of cooperation and collaboration across cultures, communities, and nations. It promotes the ability to work collaboratively with others, appreciate diverse viewpoints, and seek common ground to address global challenges. It encourages students to recognize the interdependence of nations and to find shared solutions.

Ethical Decision-Making: Global citizenship education guides students in developing ethical decision-making skills. It encourages students to consider the ethical implications of their choices and actions, and to make decisions that align with values such as justice, fairness, and sustainability. It promotes a sense of personal integrity and responsible decision-making.

Civic Engagement: Global citizenship education promotes active civic engagement at local, national, and global levels. It encourages students to participate in democratic processes, advocate for social change, and engage in community service and volunteering. It fosters a sense of agency and encourages students to take an active role in shaping their communities and the world.

By embedding these values in global citizenship education, students develop a strong ethical foundation and acquire the skills and attitudes necessary to navigate an increasingly interconnected and interdependent world. These values provide a framework for students to become responsible, informed, and engaged global citizens committed to creating a more just, peaceful, and sustainable world.

IX

Integrating Values From Sustainable Development Goals in the Collegiate Curriculum

Integrating the Sustainable Development Goals (SDGs) into the curriculum is an effective way to educate students about global challenges and empower them to contribute to sustainable development. By integrating the SDGs into the curriculum, students gain a deeper understanding of global challenges and develop the knowledge, skills, and attitudes needed to contribute to sustainable development. This integration helps students become active global citizens who are equipped to address complex social, economic, and environmental issues.

The Sustainable Development Goals (SDGs) are underpinned by a set of core values that guide their implementation and promote sustainable development worldwide. These values include:

Equality and Inclusion: The SDGs prioritize equality and inclusion by striving to ensure that all individuals, regardless of their gender, age, ethnicity, socioeconomic status, or disability, have equal access to resources, opportunities, and benefits. They aim to reduce inequalities and promote social justice, leaving no one behind.

Sustainability: The SDGs embrace the value of sustainability by promoting actions that meet the needs of the present without compromising the ability of future generations to meet their own needs. They emphasize the importance of balancing economic growth, social development, and environmental protection to create a more sustainable and resilient world.

Human Rights: The SDGs are deeply rooted in human rights principles and values. They recognize that sustainable development cannot be achieved without promoting and protecting human rights, including civil, political, economic, social, and cultural rights. The goals aim to ensure that all individuals can enjoy a life of dignity, freedom, and well-being.

Global Solidarity: The SDGs emphasize the importance of global solidarity in addressing global challenges. They acknowledge that sustainable development requires international cooperation, partnerships, and collective action. The goals promote collaboration among countries, organizations, and individuals to address shared problems and achieve common objectives.

Accountability and Transparency: The SDGs emphasize accountability and transparency at all levels. They call for monitoring progress, tracking indicators, and reporting on achievements and challenges. They promote the active participation of governments, civil society, and other stakeholders in decision-making processes and ensure that actions are taken with transparency and integrity.

Participation and Empowerment: The SDGs value the participation and empowerment of all individuals and communities. They recognize that sustainable development can only be achieved through the active engagement of people at all levels. The goals promote inclusive and participatory processes that empower individuals and communities to contribute to decision-making, implementation, and monitoring of sustainable development initiatives.

Peace and Security: The SDGs acknowledge the interlinkages between sustainable development and peace. They recognize that sustainable development is not possible without peace, and peace is not sustainable without development. The goals promote peaceful and inclusive societies, access to justice, and strong institutions as key enablers of sustainable development.

Ethical and Responsible Conduct: The SDGs uphold ethical and responsible conduct in achieving sustainable development. They emphasize the importance of responsible consumption and production, ethical business practices, and the protection of natural resources and ecosystems. The goals promote a sense of responsibility towards the planet and future generations.

By embodying these values, the SDGs provide a comprehensive framework for addressing the most pressing challenges facing humanity and the planet. They guide governments, organizations, and individuals in their efforts to build a more equitable, sustainable, and prosperous future for all.

X

Integrating Social Innovation Framework into the Graduate School Curriculum

Integrating a social innovation framework into the curriculum can help students develop the skills, mindset, and knowledge necessary to create positive social change. By integrating a social innovation framework into the curriculum, students can develop critical thinking, problem-solving, collaboration, empathy, and creativity skills. They learn to tackle social challenges and become agents of positive change in their communities and beyond.

Social innovation is guided by a set of values that underpin its principles and practices. These values shape the way social innovators approach problems, design solutions, and engage with stakeholders. Here are some values commonly embedded in social innovation:

Social Impact: Social innovation is driven by a strong commitment to creating positive social change. It emphasizes the value of improving the well-being and quality of life for individuals, communities, and society as a whole. The focus is on addressing social problems, reducing inequalities, and generating meaningful and sustainable impact.

Empathy and Human-Centeredness: Social innovation values empathy and a human-centered approach. It recognizes the importance of understanding the needs, aspirations, and experiences of the people affected by social challenges. By empathizing with individuals and communities, social innovators can design solutions that are responsive, relevant, and respectful of the people they aim to serve.

Collaboration and Co-creation: Collaboration is a key value in social innovation. It recognizes that addressing complex social problems requires collective efforts and diverse perspectives. Social innovators actively engage and collaborate with stakeholders, including community members, organizations, government agencies, and experts, to co-create solutions that draw on a range of knowledge, resources, and expertise.

Inclusion and Equity: Social innovation promotes inclusion and equity as fundamental values. It seeks to ensure that marginalized and disadvantaged groups have a voice, representation, and equal access to opportunities and resources. It strives to address systemic inequalities and promote social justice by designing solutions that are inclusive and equitable.

Openness and Adaptability: Social innovation values openness to new ideas, approaches, and ways of thinking. It encourages learning from both successes and failures, and it embraces experimentation and adaptability. Social innovators are willing to challenge existing norms and systems, and they continuously iterate and improve their solutions based on feedback and changing circumstances.

Sustainability and Systems Thinking: Social innovation recognizes the interconnectedness and complexity of social, economic, and environmental systems. It values a long-term perspective and aims to create solutions that are environmentally sustainable, economically viable, and socially beneficial. Social innovators consider the broader system and unintended consequences to design interventions that address root causes and create lasting change.

Ethical Practice and Responsible Innovation: Social innovation upholds ethical principles and responsible practices. It emphasizes integrity, transparency, and accountability in all stages of the innovation process. Social innovators consider the ethical implications of their actions, ensure informed consent and privacy, and strive to minimize potential harms and risks.

Empowerment and Capacity Building: Social innovation values the empowerment of individuals and communities. It aims to build their capacity to participate actively in shaping solutions and driving change. Social innovators support the development of skills, knowledge, and resources within communities, enabling them to take ownership of their own solutions and drive sustainable impact.

Learning and Continuous Improvement: Social innovation embraces a learning mindset and a commitment to continuous improvement. It values ongoing reflection, evaluation, and learning from experiences and outcomes. Social innovators seek to deepen their understanding of social issues, refine their approaches, and share knowledge and best practices with others.

By embracing these values, social innovation fosters a holistic and ethical approach to addressing social challenges. It promotes a vision of a more inclusive, equitable, and sustainable society, and it empowers individuals and communities to actively participate in creating positive change.

References

Andrzejewska, J., Czerkawska, J., & Manojlović, B. (Eds.). (2018). Global Education in Europe: Policies, Practices, and Theories. Palgrave Macmillan.

Aoki, N., & Kuwahara, T. (Eds.). (2018). Education for Sustainable Development Goals: Learning Objectives. United Nations University Institute for the Advanced Study of Sustainability.

Brown, T. (2009). Change by Design: How Design Thinking Transforms Organizations and Inspires Innovation. HarperBusiness.

Brown, T., & Wyatt, J. (2010). Design Thinking for Social Innovation. Stanford Social Innovation Review, 8(1), 30-35.

Ferriter, W. M., Anderson, M., & Schneider, J. K. (2015). The Responsive Classroom: Teaching That Fosters Equity and Belonging. Center for Responsive Schools.

Lickona, T. (1992). Educating for Character: How Our Schools Can Teach Respect and Responsibility. Bantam Books.

Lickona, T. (2004). Character Matters: How to Help Our Children Develop Good Judgment, Integrity, and Other Essential Virtues. Touchstone.

Liedtka, J. (2015). Perspective: Linking Design Thinking with Innovation Outcomes through Cognitive Bias Reduction. Journal of Product Innovation Management, 32(6), 925-938.

Martin, R., & Osberg, S. (2007). Social Entrepreneurship: The Case for Definition. Stanford Social Innovation Review, 5(2), 28-39.

Mulgan, G. (2006). Social Innovation: What It Is, Why It Matters and How It Can Be Accelerated. The Young Foundation. Retrieved from https://youngfoundation.org/wp-content/uploads/2012/10/Social-Innovation-by-Geoff-Mulgan.pdf

Oxfam. (2015). Education for Global Citizenship: A Guide for Schools. Retrieved from https://policy-practice.oxfam.org.uk/publications/education-for-global-citizenship-a-guide-for-schools-338547

Reimers, F., & Chung, C. K. (Eds.). (2016). Teaching and Learning for the Sustainable Future. UNESCO.

Rizvi, F., & Lingard, B. (2010). Globalizing Education Policy. Routledge.

Strike, K. A., & Soltis, J. F. (2004). The Ethics of Teaching: A Casebook. Teachers College Press.

Tomlinson, C. A. (2000). The Differentiated School: Making Revolutionary Changes in Teaching and Learning. ASCD.

United Nations Educational, Scientific and Cultural Organization (UNESCO). (2014). Global Citizenship Education: Topics and Learning Objectives. Retrieved from http://unesdoc.unesco.org/images/0023/002329/232993E.pdf

United Nations. (2015). Transforming our world: The 2030 Agenda for Sustainable Development. Retrieved from https://sdgs.un.org/2030agenda

Westley, F., Zimmerman, B., & Patton, M. (2006). Getting to Maybe: How the World Is Changed. Vintage Canada.

Wilson, J., Schubert, W. H., & Pinar, W. F. (Eds.). (1999). Teaching Values: Critical Perspectives on Education, Politics, and Culture. Routledge.

Free Module:

UNDERSTANDING AND ENHANCING SELF-REFLECTION

Teachers' Module on Metacognitive Thinking

by

Dr. Bernardo C. Lunar &
Dr. Ma. Socorro M. Eala

April 2023

Module Overview:

The Metacognitive Thinking module provides an in-depth exploration of metacognition and its role in self-reflection and learning. Metacognition refers to our ability to think about our own thinking processes, monitor our cognitive activities, and regulate our learning strategies. This module aims to enhance participants' metacognitive skills, empowering them to become more self-aware, effective learners and critical thinkers.

Learning Objectives:

1. Define metacognition and its importance in learning and problem-solving.
2. Understand the components of metacognitive thinking, including metacognitive knowledge and metacognitive regulation.
3. Recognize the benefits of metacognitive thinking for personal and academic growth.
4. Develop strategies for enhancing metacognitive skills and self-reflection.
5. Apply metacognitive thinking techniques to improve learning,

decision-making, and problem-solving processes.

Module Outline:

I. Introduction to Metacognitive Thinking

Definition and overview of metacognition

Importance of metacognitive thinking in learning and problem-solving

II. Components of Metacognitive Thinking

Metacognitive knowledge: Declarative, procedural, and conditional knowledge

Metacognitive regulation: Planning, monitoring, and evaluating cognitive processes

III. Benefits of Metacognitive Thinking

Improved self-awareness and self-regulation

Enhanced learning and retention of information

Enhanced critical thinking and problem-solving abilities

IV. Strategies for Enhancing Metacognitive Skills (30 minutes)

Reflection techniques: Journaling, self-questioning, and self-explanation

Goal setting and planning

Monitoring and self-assessment strategies

V. Application of Metacognitive Thinking

Applying metacognitive thinking in learning: Reading, note-taking, and studying

Metacognition in decision-making and problem-solving

Real-life examples and case studies

VI. Constructing Metacognitive-based Instructional Materials
Additional Resources:

Recommended readings and further references on metacognition
Online resources and tools for enhancing metacognitive skills

Assessment:

- To gauge participants' understanding and application of metacognitive thinking, consider incorporating the following assessment methods:
- Quizzes or short assessments during the module
- Group or individual activities where participants can apply metacognitive thinking strategies
- Post-module reflections or assignments to reinforce learning and encourage self-reflection

A. Introduction to Metacognitive Thinking

In this section, the module provides an overview of metacognition and highlights its significance in the processes of learning and problem-solving. The following details can be covered during this introduction:

Definition of Metacognition:

Metacognition can be defined as the ability to think about our own thinking processes. It involves being aware of our cognitive activities, monitoring them, and regulating them effectively.

Metacognitive thinking goes beyond the content of what we are learning or thinking about; it focuses on the process of how we acquire knowledge, comprehend information, and make decisions.

Overview of Metacognitive Thinking:

- Metacognitive thinking involves two key components: metacognitive knowledge and metacognitive regulation.

- Metacognitive knowledge refers to our understanding and awareness of our cognitive processes, strategies, and abilities. It can be further categorized into three types:

1. Declarative knowledge: Knowing what we know and what we don't know. Understanding our strengths and weaknesses in different areas.

2. Procedural knowledge: Knowing how to apply different strategies and techniques for learning, problem-solving, and decision-making.

3. Conditional knowledge: Knowing when and why to use specific strategies or approaches in different contexts.

Metacognitive regulation refers to the processes we use to control and monitor our cognitive activities. It includes planning, monitoring, and evaluating our thinking and learning processes.

Importance of Metacognitive Thinking in Learning and Problem-Solving:

Metacognitive thinking plays a crucial role in effective learning and problem-solving. By being aware of our cognitive processes and strategies, we can optimize our learning experiences and outcomes.

Metacognitive thinking enables us to:

- Reflect on our learning goals and set realistic objectives.
- Plan and organize our study or problem-solving strategies.

- Monitor our understanding and progress while engaging with new information or complex problems.
- Identify and rectify any gaps or misconceptions in our knowledge.
- Evaluate the effectiveness of our learning strategies and make necessary adjustments.

Transfer our learning to new situations and apply our knowledge and skills effectively.

By providing a clear understanding of metacognition and emphasizing its importance, this introduction sets the stage for the subsequent sections that delve deeper into the components, benefits, strategies, and applications of metacognitive thinking.

B. Components of Metacognitive Thinking

This section explores the two main components of metacognitive thinking: metacognitive knowledge and metacognitive regulation. Participants will gain an understanding of the different types of metacognitive knowledge and the processes involved in metacognitive regulation. The following details can be covered in this section:

Metacognitive Knowledge:

a. Declarative Knowledge:

Declarative knowledge refers to our awareness of what we know and what we don't know. It involves recognizing our strengths and weaknesses in specific subjects or areas of knowledge. Declarative knowledge helps us identify gaps in our understanding and prioritize our learning efforts.

b. Procedural Knowledge:

Procedural knowledge relates to knowing how to apply different strategies and techniques for learning, problem-solving, and decision-making. It includes knowledge of effective study techniques, problem-solving methods, and decision-making frameworks.

Procedural knowledge allows us to select and employ appropriate strategies based on the task at hand.

c. Conditional Knowledge:

Conditional knowledge involves understanding when and why to use specific strategies or approaches in different contexts. It encompasses knowledge of the conditions under which certain strategies are most effective. Conditional knowledge enables us to adapt our strategies and approaches based on the situation or the nature of the task.

Metacognitive Regulation:

Planning refers to the process of setting goals, organizing tasks, and outlining strategies to achieve desired learning or problem-solving outcomes. Effective planning involves breaking down complex tasks into manageable steps and allocating resources effectively. Planning helps us establish a clear roadmap and structure for our cognitive activities.

Monitoring involves actively observing and assessing our own cognitive processes and performance. It includes self-awareness of our comprehension, attention, and progress while engaging with new information or solving problems. Monitoring helps us identify any gaps in understanding, detect errors, and assess the effectiveness of our strategies.

Evaluating involves critically assessing our own cognitive processes, strategies, and outcomes.

It entails reflecting on the effectiveness of our learning or problem-solving approaches and making adjustments as needed. Evaluating allows us to identify areas for improvement, recognize successful strategies, and enhance our future performance.

C. Benefits of Metacognitive Thinking

This section focuses on the various benefits that metacognitive thinking offers in personal and academic contexts. Participants will understand how metacognitive thinking positively impacts self-awareness, learning, retention of information, critical thinking, and problem-solving. The following details can be covered in this section:

Improved Self-Awareness and Self-Regulation:

Metacognitive thinking promotes self-awareness by encouraging individuals to reflect on their own thinking processes and learning strategies. It helps individuals understand their strengths and weaknesses, enabling them to capitalize on their strengths and address areas that require improvement. Metacognitive thinking enhances self-regulation by enabling individuals to monitor and adjust their cognitive processes, ensuring optimal performance and learning outcomes.

Enhanced Learning and Retention of Information:

Metacognitive thinking empowers learners to actively engage in the learning process by setting goals, selecting appropriate strategies, and monitoring their understanding. It promotes deep learning and comprehension by encouraging individuals to reflect on the meaning and significance of the information they encounter. Metacognitive thinking improves information retention by helping learners make connections, organize knowledge, and transfer learning to new contexts effectively.

Enhanced Critical Thinking and Problem-Solving Abilities:

Metacognitive thinking cultivates critical thinking skills by encouraging individuals to evaluate their own reasoning processes and consider alternative perspectives. It promotes higher-order thinking, such as analysis, synthesis, and evaluation, by guiding individuals to reflect on the reliability and validity of information. Metacognitive thinking supports effective problem-solving by enabling individuals to plan, monitor progress, and evaluate their strategies, leading to more efficient and successful outcomes.

D. Strategies for Enhancing Metacognitive Skills

This section provides participants with practical strategies for developing and enhancing their metacognitive skills. The focus is on reflection techniques, goal setting and planning, as well as monitoring and self-assessment strategies. The following details can be covered in this section:

Reflection Techniques:

a. Journaling:

Journaling involves regularly writing down thoughts, experiences, and reflections about learning or problem-solving processes. It encourages metacognitive thinking by promoting self-reflection and self-awareness. Journaling helps individuals identify patterns, clarify their thinking, and recognize areas for improvement.

b. Self-Questioning:

Self-questioning involves posing thoughtful questions to oneself during the learning or problem-solving process. It encourages individuals to engage actively with the content and consider their own understanding and reasoning. Self-questioning prompts individuals to reflect on the purpose, relevance, and connections within the material.

c. Self-Explanation:

Self-explanation involves explaining concepts, steps, or solutions to oneself using one's own words. It enhances comprehension by requiring individuals to articulate their understanding and identify any gaps or misconceptions. Self-explanation promotes deeper processing of information and strengthens memory retention.

Goal Setting and Planning:

Setting clear and specific goals helps individuals focus their efforts and direct their attention toward desired learning outcomes. Goals should be realistic, measurable, and time-bound to provide a clear sense of progress and achievement. Planning involves breaking down complex tasks into smaller, manageable steps and organizing resources effectively.

Monitoring and Self-Assessment Strategies:

Regularly monitoring one's progress and understanding throughout the learning or problem-solving process is crucial for metacognitive development. Self-assessment involves evaluating one's own performance, identifying strengths and weaknesses, and making necessary adjustments. Strategies such as checklists, progress tracking, and self-rating scales can aid in monitoring and self-assessment.

E. Application of Metacognitive Thinking

In this section, participants will explore practical applications of metacognitive thinking in various contexts, including learning, decision-making, and problem-solving. Real-life examples and case studies can be used to illustrate the relevance and effectiveness of metacognitive strategies. The following details can be covered in this section:

Applying Metacognitive Thinking in Learning:

a. Reading:

Metacognitive thinking can be applied to reading by setting reading goals, previewing the text, and activating prior knowledge. Strategies like highlighting, summarizing, and asking questions while reading enhance comprehension and retention. Reflection after reading helps consolidate learning and identify areas that require further exploration.

b. Note-Taking:

Metacognitive thinking can be applied to note-taking by using active listening skills and selecting relevant information. Strategies like summarizing, organizing information, and making connections improve understanding and retention.

Reviewing and revising notes with metacognitive reflection enhances learning and knowledge consolidation.

c. Studying:

Metacognitive thinking can be applied to studying by creating study plans, breaking down material into manageable chunks, and using appropriate learning strategies. Strategies like self-quizzing, elaboration, and spaced repetition enhance comprehension and long-term retention. Regular self-assessment and adjustment of study strategies based on performance and feedback improve study effectiveness.

Metacognition in Decision-Making and Problem-Solving:

Metacognitive thinking plays a crucial role in decision-making and problem-solving by guiding individuals to analyze and evaluate their thought processes. Identifying biases, considering alternative perspectives, and reflecting on decision-making strategies enhance critical thinking. Monitoring and evaluating problem-solving approaches, adjusting strategies, and seeking feedback promote efficient and effective problem-solving.

Real-Life Examples and Case Studies:

Real-life examples and case studies can be used to demonstrate how individuals apply metacognitive thinking in various situations. Participants can examine how successful individuals or professionals utilize metacognitive strategies to improve their learning, decision-making, and problem-solving. Analyzing real-life examples helps participants understand the practical application of metacognitive thinking and inspires them to adopt similar strategies.

F. Constructing Metacognitive-based Instructional Materials

These are the steps to follow as you develop your Metacognitive-Based Instructional Materials

1. Content Selection and Organization:

- Selecting relevant content that aligns with the learning objectives and promotes metacognitive thinking.
- Organizing the content in a logical and meaningful sequence to facilitate comprehension and application of metacognitive strategies.

2. Instructional Strategies:

- Selecting appropriate instructional strategies, such as explicit instruction, guided practice, and peer collaboration, to engage learners in metacognitive thinking.
- Incorporating varied instructional formats, such as videos, interactive activities, and discussions, to cater to different learning preferences.

3. Assessment and Feedback:

- Designing formative and summative assessments that assess both content knowledge and metacognitive skills.
- Providing constructive feedback that focuses on metacognitive processes and suggests areas for improvement.

4. Implementation and Evaluation

a. Implementation Considerations:
- Considering the context, audience, and available resources when implementing metacognitive instructional materials.
- Adapting and modifying the materials as needed to meet the specific needs of learners.

b. Evaluation of Effectiveness:
- Discussing methods to evaluate the effectiveness of metacognitive instructional materials, such as learner feedback, pre- and post-assessments, and observation.
- Using evaluation data to inform future revisions and improvements to the materials.

Appendix A

Recommended readings and further references on metacognition

These readings provide a solid foundation for understanding metacognition and its applications in various learning contexts. They offer theoretical insights, research findings, and practical strategies for promoting metacognitive thinking among learners.

"Metacognition in Learning and Instruction: Theory, Research and Practice" by Dunlosky, J. & Metcalfe, J. (Eds.) (2008) - This book explores various aspects of metacognition in educational settings, including its role in self-regulated learning, instructional strategies to promote metacognitive thinking, and the impact of metacognition on academic performance.

"Metacognitive Processes in Academic Writing: A Systematic Review of Research" by Efklides, A. (2008) - This research review focuses on metacognitive processes specifically related to academic writing, discussing the strategies employed by proficient writers and the role of metacognition in writing development.

"Developing Minds: An American Ghost Story" by Meier, H. (2015) - This book delves into the concept of metacognition and its relevance in education. It explores the author's experiences and observations in promoting metacognitive thinking among students and offers practical strategies for educators.

"Metacognition, Strategy Use, and Instruction" by Schraw, G., & Moshman, D. (Eds.) (1995) - This book provides a comprehensive exploration of metacognition, strategy use, and instructional approaches to promote metacognitive thinking in diverse learning contexts.

"Teaching Metacognition: Promoting Self-Regulation and Critical Thinking" by Lovett, M. C. (2013) - This article discusses the importance of metacognition in education and provides practical strategies for teachers to foster metacognitive skills and self-regulated learning in their students.

"Metacognition and Learning: Conceptual and Methodological Considerations" by Azevedo, R. (2009) - This article offers an overview of metacognition and its relationship to learning. It discusses conceptual and methodological considerations in metacognitive research and provides insights into instructional approaches that promote metacognitive thinking.

References

Flavell, J. H. (1979). Metacognition and cognitive monitoring: A new area of cognitive-developmental inquiry. American Psychologist, 34(10), 906-911.

Dunlosky, J., & Metcalfe, J. (Eds.). (2008). Metacognition in learning and instruction: Theory, research, and practice. Routledge.

Schraw, G., & Moshman, D. (Eds.). (1995). Metacognition, strategy use, and instruction. Lawrence Erlbaum Associates.

Brown, A. L. (1978). Knowing when, where, and how to remember: A problem of metacognition. In R. Glaser (Ed.), Advances in instructional psychology (Vol. 1, pp. 77-165). Lawrence Erlbaum Associates.

Efklides, A. (2008). Metacognition and affect: What can metacognitive experiences tell us about the learning process? Educational Research Review, 3(3), 190-199.

Lovett, M. C. (2013). Teaching metacognition: Promoting self-regulated learning and critical thinking. In V. A. Benassi, C. E. Overson, & C. M. Hakala (Eds.), Applying science of learning in education: Infusing psychological science into the curriculum (pp. 55-66). Society for the Teaching of Psychology.

Azevedo, R. (2009). Metacognition in educational settings: From theory to practice. In D. J. Hacker, J. Dunlosky, & A. C. Graesser (Eds.), Handbook of metacognition in education (pp. 1-16). Routledge.

Flavell, J. H. (1987). Speculations about the nature and development of metacognition. In F. E. Weinert & R. H. Kluwe (Eds.), Metacognition, motivation, and understanding (pp. 21-29). Lawrence Erlbaum Associates.

Zimmerman, B. J. (2002). Becoming a self-regulated learner: An overview. Theory Into Practice, 41(2), 64-70.

Pintrich, P. R. (2002). The role of metacognitive knowledge in learning, teaching, and assessing. Theory Into Practice, 41(4), 219-225.

Appendix B

Online resources and tools that can help enhance metacognitive skills

These online resources and tools provide convenient and accessible ways to develop and enhance metacognitive skills. Whether through structured online courses, digital tools for organization and reflection, or interactive platforms for discussions and self-assessment, individuals can leverage these resources to actively engage in metacognitive thinking and promote effective learning and problem-solving.

Online Learning Platforms:

Platforms like Coursera, edX, and Khan Academy offer a wide range of courses on metacognition and learning strategies. These courses provide structured content, interactive activities, and assessments to support the development of metacognitive skills.

Self-Assessment Tools:

Online self-assessment tools, such as the Metacognitive Awareness Inventory (MAI) and the Metacognitive Awareness of Reading Strategies

Inventory (MARSI), allow individuals to evaluate their metacognitive awareness and identify areas for improvement.

Mind Mapping Software:

Tools like MindMeister, XMind, and Coggle enable users to create visual mind maps that aid in organizing thoughts, making connections, and promoting metacognitive reflection.

Digital Note-Taking Tools:

Apps like Evernote, Microsoft OneNote, and Google Keep provide digital note-taking capabilities that support metacognitive strategies, such as summarizing, highlighting, and organizing information for effective studying and reviewing.

Reflection and Journaling Apps:

Applications like Reflectly, Daylio, and Journey offer digital platforms for journaling and reflective writing, providing prompts and reminders for metacognitive reflection and self-assessment.

Metacognitive Questioning Tools:

Tools like ThinkerAnalytix and Paideia Online provide platforms for generating metacognitive questions and engaging in critical thinking discussions, fostering metacognitive thinking and analysis of complex topics.

Online Study and Productivity Tools:

Tools like Trello, Asana, and Todoist help individuals plan and organize their tasks, set goals, and monitor progress. These tools support metacognitive skills such as goal setting, planning, and self-regulation.

Online Forums and Discussion Platforms:

Participating in online forums and discussion platforms, such as Reddit, Quora, or educational forums specific to the subject area, allows learners to engage in metacognitive discussions, ask questions, and gain different perspectives.
Metacognitive Apps for Students:

Mobile applications like Brainscape, Quizlet, and Anki offer flashcard-based learning with built-in metacognitive features like spaced repetition, self-quizzing, and progress tracking.
Online Metacognitive Learning Resources:

Websites like TeachThought, Edutopia, and Learning Scientists provide articles, blog posts, and resources dedicated to metacognition, offering insights, strategies, and practical tips for enhancing metacognitive skills.

Appendix C

Sample Reflection Guide

This sample reflection guide can be used to guide individuals through a structured process of reflecting on their learning experiences and engaging in metacognitive thinking. The guide can be adapted and customized based on specific learning contexts and objectives.

Introduction:

Start by explaining the purpose and importance of reflection in promoting metacognition.
Emphasize that reflection allows individuals to gain insights into their learning processes, strengths, areas for improvement, and strategies for future success.

Set the Context:

Provide a brief overview of the learning experience or task that individuals are reflecting upon. Remind participants of the learning objectives and any specific metacognitive strategies that were employed during the experience.

Description of the Experience:

Ask participants to describe the learning experience in detail, focusing on what they did, observed, and encountered during the process. Encourage them to provide specific examples and include relevant details.

Metacognitive Questions:

Pose a series of metacognitive questions to guide participants' reflection. Some sample questions include:

What were your initial thoughts and feelings about the task or learning experience?

What strategies did you use to approach the task? Were they effective?

How did you monitor your progress and adjust your strategies during the process?

Did you encounter any challenges or obstacles? How did you overcome them?

What did you learn about yourself as a learner through this experience?

What would you do differently if you were to approach a similar task or learning experience in the future?

Analysis and Evaluation:

Ask participants to analyze and evaluate their performance and learning outcomes. Encourage them to consider both successes and areas for improvement.

Prompt them to reflect on the effectiveness of the metacognitive strategies employed and whether they contributed to their learning and success.

Insights and Lessons Learned:

Encourage participants to draw insights and lessons from their reflection. What did they learn about their strengths, weaknesses, and metacognitive skills? Ask them to identify specific strategies or approaches that were effective and can be applied in future learning experiences.

Action Plan:

Based on their reflection and insights, ask participants to develop an action plan for future learning. What specific steps or strategies will they implement to enhance their metacognitive skills and improve their learning outcomes?

Conclusion:

Summarize the key points discussed during the reflection.

Highlight the value of ongoing reflection and metacognitive thinking in promoting continuous learning and growth.

*** Remember, the reflection guide should be adaptable to the specific context and learning objectives. It's important to create a safe and supportive environment that encourages participants to be open and honest in their reflections.

Appendix D

ORID Model of Focused Conversation

The ORID Model of Focused Conversation is a framework used to guide structured and meaningful conversations around a specific topic or experience. The model was developed by the Institute of Cultural Affairs (ICA) and is commonly used in group facilitation, coaching, and reflective practice. The acronym ORID stands for Objective, Reflective, Interpretive, and Decisional. Each phase of the model corresponds to a different type of question that prompts participants to engage in deeper thinking and reflection. Here's an overview of each phase:

Objective Phase:

The Objective phase focuses on gathering factual information and observations related to the topic or experience.

Key question: What are the facts, data, and observable details about the topic?

Reflective Phase:

The Reflective phase encourages participants to explore their emotions, reactions, and personal responses to the topic or experience.

Key question: How did you feel about the topic or experience? What were your initial reactions or responses?

Interpretive Phase:

The Interpretive phase invites participants to analyze and make sense of the information and emotions shared in the previous phases.

Key question: What patterns, insights, or connections can you identify from the facts and your emotional responses? What do you think is the significance or meaning of these observations?

Decisional Phase:

The Decisional phase focuses on generating action steps, making decisions, and considering potential next steps based on the insights and understanding gained through the conversation.

Key question: What actions, solutions, or decisions can be made based on the information, reflections, and interpretations? What are the next steps or implications?

By following the ORID Model, facilitators or individuals can guide a focused conversation that moves through each phase, allowing for a comprehensive exploration of a topic or experience. The model encourages participants to engage in deeper thinking, reflect on their emotions, analyze information, and generate meaningful actions or decisions. It provides a structured framework for effective communication, reflection, and problem-solving.

Appendix E

DEAL Model of Critical Reflection

The DEAL Model of Critical Reflection is a framework for engaging in reflective thinking and analysis. The model was developed by Dr. David Boud, an expert in the field of reflective practice and adult learning. DEAL stands for Description, Examination, Analysis, and Learning. Each phase of the model prompts individuals to systematically reflect on their experiences, actions, and learning. Here's an overview of each phase:

Description:

In the Description phase, individuals provide an objective and detailed account of the experience or situation they are reflecting upon. The focus is on capturing the facts, events, and key elements of the experience.

Examination:

In the Examination phase, individuals explore their thoughts, feelings, and reactions related to the experience. This phase involves analyzing and reflecting on personal responses, perspectives, and assumptions.

Analysis:

In the Analysis phase, individuals delve deeper into the experience, critically examining it from different angles and considering various factors and influences. This phase involves identifying patterns, connections, and underlying causes or implications of the experience.

Learning:

In the Learning phase, individuals draw insights and learning outcomes from their reflection, identifying key takeaways and implications for future actions or behaviors. This phase involves considering how the experience contributes to personal growth, learning, and professional development.

The DEAL Model provides a structured approach to critical reflection, guiding individuals through a process of systematically exploring their experiences, examining their thoughts and feelings, analyzing the situation, and deriving meaningful learning outcomes. It helps individuals gain deeper insights into their actions and experiences, fostering personal and professional development.

www.ingramcontent.com/pod-product-compliance
Lightning Source LLC
LaVergne TN
LVHW050333160826
845677LV00014B/3613
* 9 7 8 6 2 1 4 7 0 7 9 9 7 *